Making Meetings Work
How to Plan and Conduct Effective Meetings

Karen Anderson

American Media Publishing
4900 University Avenue
West Des Moines, Iowa 50266-6769
1-800-262-2557

Making Meetings Work:
How to Plan and Conduct Effective Meetings

Karen Anderson
Copyright © 1994 by National Press Publications
A Division of Rockhurst College Continuing Education Center, Inc.

This publication is designed to provide accurate and authoritative information in regard to the subject matter covered. It is sold with the understanding that neither the author nor the publisher is engaged in rendering legal, accounting, or other professional service. If legal advice or other expert assistance is required, the services of a competent professional should be sought.

American Media Publishing:

Managing Editor:
Designer:
Cover design:

Art Bauer
Todd McDonald
Karen Massetti Miller
Gayle O'Brien
Maura Rombalski

This publication was developed from the book *To Meet or Not to Meet* written by Karen Anderson, published by National Press Publications, a Division of Rockhurst College Continuing Education Center, Inc.

Published by American Media Inc.
4900 University Avenue
West Des Moines, IA 50266-6769

Library of Congress Catalog Card Number 94-71156
Anderson, Karen
Making Meetings Work

Printed in the United States of America
1999
ISBN 1-884926-20-7

Introduction

When both your mind and body go numb, when your ears refuse to listen a second longer, and when your next yawn makes you realize you really are awake but wish you weren't—that's when you know you're in another boring, endless meeting. Most meetings occur too often, last too long, and accomplish too little.

Whether you attend meetings as a participant or a leader, you are investing your time, presence, preparation, and concentration. Your investment may also include your reputation—the skill with which you plan, conduct, and contribute to meetings. This skill requires confidence and competence in multiple areas, such as organization, leadership, time management, space management, problem solving, conflict resolution, oral and written communication, group dynamics, and training strategies.

Gulp!

This list seems overwhelming, yet you already perform with reasonable confidence and competence in all these areas in your everyday tasks. Just consider how you manage a family and a home! Managing a household is a more complicated job than managing a meeting, but you don't think of it as anything exceptional. Yet, those skills are the same you'll use for running effective meetings, and running effective meetings is an exceptional skill. Your numb limbs and wide yawns in the last meeting attest to that!

You embark on an adventure each time you manage a meeting. Knowing how to save time, effort, and money for your company by having fewer, shorter, and better meetings is definitely to your career advantage. Check the following objectives and add any that you especially want to focus on while using this handbook.

Objectives

◆ To save time by holding only necessary meetings, by starting and ending meetings at agreed times, and by asking people to prepare or know background material prior to the meeting.

◆ To communicate better the first time, encourage team collaboration, and use company resources, such as personnel and property, as efficiently and effectively as possible.

◆ To save effort by preparing essential materials before any decisions must be made.

While pursuing those objectives, you'll experience some additional advantages.

Advantages

◆ Increased self-awareness, self-confidence, and visibility in order to save time and be more productive.

◆ Improved communications skills, leadership skills, and organizational skills.

Special Note

As you use this handbook, highlight tips you want to include in your repertoire of strategies and skills. Keep a personal index of comments and references on the Table of Contents page, and concentrate on one chapter at a time. You can learn to manage meetings that occur just often enough, last just long enough, and accomplish more than enough. The guidesheets, tips, and examples included are practical steps to make planning meetings easy.

Chapter *One*

Assessing Your Meeting Needs

Chapter Objectives

▶ Recognize the HIDDEN agenda you should bring to your meetings.

▶ Use the Four-P Needs Assessment to determine your meeting needs.

Determining how well you currently plan and run meetings will provide you with a point of reference for improvement. Use the Self-Assessment Survey on the following pages to identify your strengths and establish areas in which you can improve.

In this first chapter, you'll build a firm foundation for preparing your next meeting. Assessing, planning, promoting, organizing, and rehearsing both the context and the content of a meeting for a specific audience are essential for assuring a successful meeting. Let's begin with assessing.

You embark on an adventure each time you manage a meeting.

You embark on an adventure each time you manage a meeting. Knowing how to save time, effort, and money for your company by having fewer, shorter, and better meetings is definitely to your advantage. Check the following objectives, and add any that you especially want to focus on while using this handbook.

Self-Assessment Survey

Answer each item by checking the most representative column: Often, Sometimes, or Seldom. Your honest answer is the "right answer."

1

		Often	Sometimes	Seldom
1.	I schedule time on my daily calendar to prepare for a meeting.	[ ]	[ ]	[ ]
2.	I plan only essential meetings whose purposes cannot be achieved in other ways.	[ ]	[ ]	[ ]
3.	I set meeting objectives that are compatible with project goals and official company statements.	[ ]	[ ]	[ ]
4.	I send both meeting announcements and agenda surveys to participants well in advance.	[ ]	[ ]	[ ]
5.	I ask for attendance confirmation and/or make reminder memos or calls prior to the meeting day.	[ ]	[ ]	[ ]
6.	I arrange documentation for the meeting in advance.	[ ]	[ ]	[ ]
7.	I prepare materials needed for the meeting well in advance.	[ ]	[ ]	[ ]
8.	I arrange for appropriate space for the meeting well in advance.	[ ]	[ ]	[ ]
9.	I have a list of phone numbers for participants.	[ ]	[ ]	[ ]

continued

Self-Assessment Survey

	Often	Sometimes	Seldom
10. I ask participants to do something specific to prepare for the meeting, such as reading a report or bringing two quality-assurance ideas.	[ ]	[ ]	[ ]
11. I rehearse my presentation and test any media equipment well in advance.	[ ]	[ ]	[ ]
12. I analyze the audience's profile before the meeting.	[ ]	[ ]	[ ]
13. I use both visual and audio aids.	[ ]	[ ]	[ ]
14. I listen without interrupting.	[ ]	[ ]	[ ]
15. I practice conflict resolution and use these communication skills to run meetings smoothly.	[ ]	[ ]	[ ]
16. I involve participants within the first few minutes of a meeting.	[ ]	[ ]	[ ]
17. I am comfortable with a pause after a question in a meeting.	[ ]	[ ]	[ ]
18. I begin the next agenda at the end of this meeting.	[ ]	[ ]	[ ]
19. I make progress checks between meetings.	[ ]	[ ]	[ ]
20. I evaluate the process and my performance after each meeting.	[ ]	[ ]	[ ]

If you answered Often to 10 or more items in the Self-Assessment Survey, you are currently preparing for meetings better than your peers. If you answered Sometimes or Seldom five or more times, your meeting preparation needs tuning.

From this survey, you probably noticed how preparation plays a key role in your effectiveness as a meeting leader. Preparing space, materials, topics, schedules, equipment, and participants is too often neglected. Even more important is your attitude about the meeting.

Your HIDDEN Agenda

Creating a welcome and warm atmosphere in which people can meet and work is crucial to the success of any meeting. Constructive meetings grow out of positive and productive interactions among members of your team. How you support each individual's efforts determines how well your meeting works, and how each member will enjoy and encourage one another. This intent is your HIDDEN Agenda:

◆ Honesty

◆ Integrity

◆ Dignity

◆ Development

◆ Empowerment

◆ Needs satisfaction

Honesty

Most people rate *honesty* high on their list of personal values. Consider these statements made by adults in the workforce:

■ "All I want is to be treated fairly and honestly."
■ "I expect my boss and my peers to be truthful with me."
■ "Honesty is the only healthy policy."
■ "Trust is built on honest, open communication."
■ "Being honest is no excuse for being mean."
■ "Gentle honesty moves me farther faster than harsh honesty does."
■ "Building rapport in a team begins with sincere caring and sharing."

> Honesty is the best policy; but he who is governed by that maxim is not an honest man.
> *Richard Whately, Archbishop of Dublin*

In a recent survey of more than 2,000 business leaders, 87% said they make judgments about people's management ability based on how well they run meetings.

If honesty is important in your work relationships, include it in your HIDDEN Agenda for each meeting. Ask for honest feedback on the agenda items. When a comment from a coworker indicates that a topic needs more time than you originally assigned to it, add the time or arrange to discuss it at another specific time. This kind of concern and commitment will do more to increase productivity than any other single factor. Studies show that people respond favorably to fair, consistent treatment. This favorable response is a great way to start a meeting.

Integrity

Integrity is closely related to honesty. Standing up for your beliefs is a healthy way of asserting your vision and objectives. Asking each participant before or during a meeting what she or he thinks about the topic at hand assures your team that your meetings rely on open discussion. When integrity is respected, creativity abounds. Integrity fosters self-esteem. High self- and team esteem and high productivity are direct results of your HIDDEN Agenda.

Dignity

Dignity helps maintain the rapport you have developed through honesty and integrity. You want your meetings to be productive interactions. Your participants want to be free from sarcasm, humiliation, intimidation, and discrimination. They want you to protect their egos and you want them to project their ideas. It's an even trade. A few examples follow:

♦ Humor works best when it is relevant to a meeting. If the purpose of your meeting is to brainstorm ways to improve customer service, then sketching a spiraling storm over each participant's corporate photograph is funny. But singling out one person's photograph with the sketch is discriminatory and may be perceived as a criticism of that person's thinking ability. Likewise, sarcasm and exaggeration may backfire. Saying, "Pat would run over anyone who got between him and a new sales account," may offend Pat or anyone else in the meeting. Most of us do not concentrate or contribute well once someone has been offended. Humor that attacks human dignity or that is racist, sexist, or sacrilegious should be avoided.

◆ Discussing specific observations and behaviors in a meeting without naming an individual will save her or him from embarrassment. Avoid statements such as "Shirley's newsletter is a waste of paper. Dumping it would give more paper to the other departments." A better way to discuss redistributing the paper supply would be, "If all departments conserve five reams of paper during the next month, we will have enough paper for the rest of the year." With a general call for conservation, Shirley may be persuaded to limit the remaining issues of the newsletter!

◆ Individual performance reviews, warnings, and firings are never appropriate in a public meeting. Were you ever reprimanded in public by a teacher or a parent? Remember the humiliation you felt? When conducting your meetings, focus on positive behaviors for the public view. Save negative behaviors for private review. You will uphold dignity by maintaining privacy.

Development

Most people thrive in an atmosphere of honesty, integrity, and dignity. This atmosphere is conducive to *development,* both personal and professional. Your meetings will be most effective when you make self- and team development part of your HIDDEN Agenda. Studies show that companies benefit the most from employees who set self-development goals, and who list measurable, reasonable plans for achieving those goals. If the participants in your next meeting are faced with a dilemma, challenge them to set personal goals that will advance the company's goals. Encourage collaboration by recognizing strengths. For instance, "Briana, you're studying warehouse management in your degree program, aren't you? Would you be willing to help our shipping and receiving department identify risk-management concerns? Your opinion would be appreciated."

A sense of humor is not so much the ability to appreciate humorous stories as it is the capacity to recognize the absurdity of the positions one gets into from time to time, together with skill in retreating from them with dignity.
Dana L. Farnsworth

An estimated 20 million business meetings take place in America every day.

Look for ways in your meetings to link company goals to a participant's development. Ask Gene to report on his experiences at the annual convention and to state how your company might use what he learned. Ask Sandra and Phil if they'd act as proofreaders for the secretarial pool when deadlines are tight. Encourage and expect people to volunteer for cross-training when their work orders relax. This cooperative spirit and personal recognition will build rapport within your team. Meetings will be pleasurable experiences when you create opportunities for participants to help one another grow.

Empowerment

Empowerment convinces members of your team that they can handle the challenges that arise. Once a problem is identified in the meeting, expect your team members to resolve it, and then do everything you can to meet their needs so they have the authority and resources to solve the problem.

Encourage risk-taking in your meetings by redefining failure as a step toward success. The biggest successes often come from taking the biggest risks. Many failures miss being successes because someone gave up too soon.

Let your meetings create future successes. If a report is incomplete in one meeting, ask the writer for a completion date and for an oral summary at another meeting, or ask for a written summary to be sent to all participants prior to the next meeting. Don't worry about people taking advantage of missing one meeting's deadline. They'll be grateful that you are willing to accommodate uncontrollable factors that interfere in their professional lives. Your attention and public recognition that the report is still expected to be completed are enough in most cases to get people on track. People typically perform well when given the space and time to show what they can do.

A quality-assurance director in a large package-labeling plant explained how he empowers his staff and controls latecomers in his meetings. Lee uses a smile upon their arrival and these words: "I'm glad you're here!" Frequently, latecomers start to tell him their excuse for being gone. He says that an explanation is not necessary, that he trusts their judgment. He finishes with, "Let's get to work." Employees are empowered to make their own decisions and live with the consequences of those decisions. Lee's staff has no need to abuse his trust, and he has no need to abuse theirs. They show up on time. This is a rare situation in most companies, but it need not be rare in your meetings. Trust participants to be there when the meeting starts. If they're not there at the beginning, begin without them and trust that they have a reason for being late or absent. If you accept that attitude, people will willingly check in with you about what they missed and what they can do to prepare for the next meeting.

Needs Satisfaction

Every meeting should have a purpose and a plan that meets participant needs. Otherwise, the meeting is a waste of time. Consider canceling a meeting if you have only general information on the agenda; send out a memo instead. You have seen how honesty, integrity, dignity, development, and empowerment fit into the HIDDEN Agenda. *Needs satisfaction* summarizes these criteria: meet your team's needs during the meetings, and members will meet your company's needs as best they know how. Actually, that's just about all any of us asks! With the six criteria in your HIDDEN Agenda, you'll have meetings that occur just often enough, that last just long enough, and that accomplish more than enough. Your investment in meeting preparation will keep your audience awake and waiting for more.

> **Every meeting should have a purpose and a plan that meets participant needs.**

The Four-P Needs Assessment

The Four-P Needs Assessment below will guide you in deciding the fate and fortune of every meeting. Will the meeting evolve into a worthwhile use of space and time with a purpose, participants, property, and a plan? If any of the four Ps is missing, consider instead a memo, a facsimile, or a phone call with the interested parties.

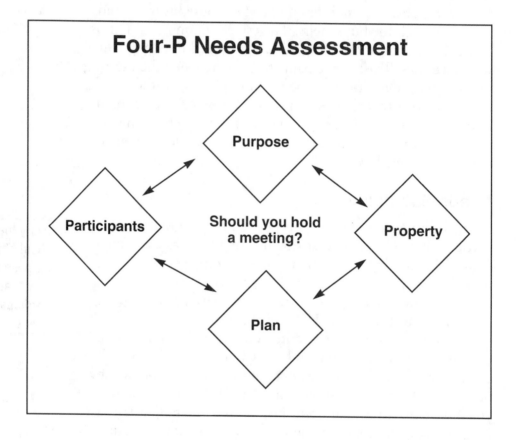

Four-P Needs Assessment

Purpose

Participants

Should you hold a meeting?

Property

Plan

Four-P Needs Assessment

Answer the questions in the four categories to determine if a meeting is necessary.

Purpose:

What are the current opportunities, conflicts, problems, concerns, or time frames that a meeting could address?

What work and decisions must be completed before the meeting?

What information needs to be distributed?

What work or decisions must be completed during the meeting?

Property:

What resources, facilities, materials, information, or equipment are needed to accomplish the meeting's goal?

Participants:

Who are the people concerned with the meeting's agenda?

Who needs to do the work or make the decisions concerning the agenda?

Who needs this information?

Who needs to be present at the meeting?

Plan:

Could this work and decisions be accomplished through any of these alternative communications?

- Memos, letters, or reports
- Facsimiles
- Electronic mail
- Voice mail or telephone calls
- Teleconferences
- Videotapes
- Satellite conferences
- Individual conversations

◆ **If any of the Ps are missing, you're not ready to conduct a meeting.**
Consider postponing or eliminating the meeting until you have the reasons and the resources for people to meet with one another.

◆ **If all of the Ps are present, a meeting is necessary!**
Begin to plan your meeting with Chapter 2.

Chapter*Two*

Planning the Meeting

Chapter Objectives

▶ Determine the purpose for having a meeting.

▶ State your meeting objectives.

▶ Plan a meeting agenda.

Congratulations! You have already saved time that is typically wasted by coming up with a well-organized plan for bringing people together. Working toward quality meetings by minimizing the number and length of meetings when possible eliminates major frustration in the workplace.

Industry Week reports that the estimated cost of wasted time in unproductive meetings exceeds $37 billion annually.

Estimates suggest that managers spend between one-fourth and one-half of their workweek sitting in meetings or preparing for them, and one-third of that time is wasted. Well-planned meetings could save at least 20 minutes in a one-hour meeting or six hours and 40 minutes in a week! Consider the participants' pay for the time you can save and you'll have a sense of the money you can save. Eliminating meetings when possible also eliminates travel time and expenses, room and equipment costs, and preparation time, as well as unproductive transition time that accompanies every meeting. Wise documentation of these savings in dollars and hours will be a real advantage on your next performance appraisal!

Knowing the primary purpose of a meeting will help you identify the kind of meeting to prepare. Here are four key purposes.

Four Purposes of Meetings

◆ To *inform*—to get or to give information

◆ To *form*—to make a decision or to solve a problem

◆ To *perform*—to complete a task

◆ To *conform*—to maintain a routine or a standard image

2

The Inform Meeting

The focus of the inform meeting is its content. The participants learn the presented information, or you learn the requested information from the participants. Usually, the inform meeting uses discussion, queries, demonstrations, briefings, and lecture to exchange information. Such a meeting usually can accommodate large groups of 10 or more participants.

The Form Meeting

The emphasis of the form meeting is the identification of concerns and the resolution of a conflict or a problem. Often, this kind of meeting uses discussion, brainstorming, persuasion, and evaluation for developing a strategic plan. A group of three to nine participants works best in this meeting, because you need enough minds to create options, recognize probable consequences, test the criteria, and select the best option. But too many people can result in indecision and denial. Odd-numbered groups avoid tie votes. Both the size and the nature of this meeting lead to creative choices and realistic resolutions.

The Perform Meeting

The perform meeting centers on working as a team to get a task done. It may be a process, such as an evaluation, or a product, such as a flowchart. This kind of meeting lends itself to application, simulation, and assignment. This work session should focus on the desired results and the desired time frame. Small groups work best and may meet interdependently, with each group working on a selected aspect of the task. The key to success in work meetings is to minimize duplication or misunderstanding through clear communication among groups. Your position as meeting leader is to act as a communications liaison.

The Conform Meeting

The conform meeting is a combination of the other three kinds of meetings. The focus is often status quo. Few people function at their highest level in a conform meeting. This kind of meeting seems to have more of a script than an agenda. If the participants are comfortable with this meeting, it may serve more as a social function than a business function. At its best, the conform meeting will develop a sense of identity and unity among participants that other kinds of meetings may not accomplish as well. Networking often evolves from this type of meeting. But don't fool yourself about its purpose!

All four types of meetings have their benefits and their limits. To help you determine which one suits your current needs, compare the Four-P Needs Assessment with the Meeting Summary Chart that follows.

Meeting Summary Chart

Four Kinds	Primary Purpose	Focus	Size of Group
Inform Meeting	Giving and/or getting information	Content (learning)	Small or large groups (2–100 participants)
Form Meeting	Making decisions or solving problems	Resolution (thinking)	Small or multiple groups (3–9 per group and 2–4 groups)
Perform Meeting	Completing a task	Results (doing)	Small or multiple groups (2–6 per group and 2–4 groups)
Conform Meeting	Maintaining a standard (being)	Tradition/ image	Small or large group (3–50 participants)

Now that you have determined the kind of meeting you need, you can turn your attention to the elements of the meeting.

Five Elements of a Meeting

◆ **Greeting**
How you welcome the participants as they arrive.

◆ **Opening**
How you introduce the presenters, leaders, the objective, the
agenda, and the instructions.

◆ **Delivery**
How you present the content or concern, or how you
organize the task.

◆ **Closing**
How you summarize decisions, make assignments, list
recommendations, set deadlines, and create action.

◆ **Feedback**
How you record the meeting, evaluate the process, and
check the progress of the items identified in the closing.

Each of these elements is detailed in the following chapters. This
brief overview gives you an idea of what to expect as you plan
your meeting.

To continue preparing for your meeting, begin with the agenda.
The Four-P Needs Assessment provides you with your starting
point. What is it that you want to accomplish during the
meeting? The answer to this question is your objective. The
most productive meeting centers on one objective that avoids
confusion and focuses your attention.

Three Guidelines for Stating Objectives of Meetings

◆ **Be specific and concrete.**
What needs to be done by when and how and where.

◆ **Be positive and optimistic.**
Expect success and avoid using negatives, such as *not* and
never.

◆ **Be realistic and practical.**
Set an objective that is attainable and measurable.

Examples

■ To improve safety at our main plant, each shift supervisor will recommend plans that can be implemented within one week for under $100 in total expenditures.

■ To improve morale in the finance department, all participants will brainstorm 20 ways to build team spirit during the next 30 days.

■ To conduct more effective meetings, each participant will evaluate his or her four most recent meetings based on criteria determined during the meeting.

With a clearly stated meeting objective, participants know the task at hand and assemble with a minimum of confusion and frustration. Some meetings have open-ended objective statements so the participants can help identify the specific criteria and/or concrete results of the meeting. However, the more complete your objective statement is, the more focused your meeting will be.

Communicating Your Objectives

The more complete your objective statement is, the more focused your meeting will be.

Once you have your meeting objective, pose it as a question to the group, rather than a command. Normally, we would all rather give answers than follow orders. When people are given choices, their personal investment in the outcome of a meeting rises. From that point, success is just a matter of time! Look at how the previous objective statements become welcome questions:

■ What plans can we implement for under $100 to improve the safety at our main plant?

■ What are 20 immediate ways of improving morale in our finance department?

■ What are your criteria for determining effective meetings, what is your evaluation of the past four meetings, and what are your top two recommendations for changes?

Once your objective becomes a question, ask yourself if the answer is realistic for the time constraints. For instance, are five plans reasonable? If not, go for two or three. Are 20 ways reasonable? If not, go for 10 or 12.

The number of participants that you invite to the meeting will impact the amount of time it takes to complete the task. The more people invited, the more ideas suggested and the more time required. Now you are ready for the Agenda Planning Worksheet.

Agenda Planning Worksheet

What *objective* is to be accomplished?

What *background* will explain the rationale for the objective?

What *questions* need answers?

Estimate *how long* it will take to get these answers.

(Include one-minute transitions and breaks as you shift from one agenda question to the next.)

1._____? Number of minutes:_____
                                Transition minute(s):_____

2._____? Number of minutes:_____
                                Transition minute(s):_____

3._____? Number of minutes:_____
                                Transition minute(s):_____

Total: _____agenda items   Total:____hours_____min.

You have enough information identified now to type a tentative agenda, such as the one below:

Tentative Agenda

Objective:	To increase the effectiveness of our information meetings. (2 min.)
Background:	Lost time and effort are costly. The budget for this year is tight. Let's conserve expenses to protect our positions. Let's reduce frustration and confusion to project a winning team.

Agenda:

What are the most important criteria for determining effectiveness in our meetings? (10 min.)

What scale would best rate these criteria? (5 min.)

How have our last four meetings rated on this scale? (7 min.)

How can our meetings be changed to make them more effective? (8 min.)

What are the two best recommendations for changes in our next meeting? (8 min.)

Total agenda items: 5   **Total time plus transitions: 40 minutes**

Preparing a tentative agenda gives you a good idea of how much time you need to accomplish the stated objective and address agenda items. Given this information, which meeting mode will work best? The three most common modes are time sensitive.

Three Common Meeting Modes

2

- The *stand-up mode* allows participants to stand for the meeting, which is usually less than 15 minutes in length. Most people don't mind standing for a few minutes, and they sometimes welcome the change in perspective from sitting behind a desk. This is also called the "no" meeting: no coffee, no cookies, no chairs!

- The *sit-down mode* allows participants to sit for the meeting, which is usually 15 to 60 minutes in length. Most adults can sit for approximately an hour before needing a break to move around, although we all know exceptions to this rule. There are days when even 20 minutes of concentration is difficult for the best of us!

- The *move-around mode* permits participants to physically and periodically adjust their seating positions. Normally, strategic shifts in agenda items will provide natural opportunities for body shifts as well. Any meeting that lasts more than an hour must have accommodations for movement: a variety of tasks, training techniques, audio-visual aids, and at least a 10-minute break for every 60 to 75 minutes the participants must sit. By getting the kinks out of the bodies, you also get the kinks out of the minds.

One more factor to consider in planning your meeting is figuring out the best time to meet. A few guidelines will help you know when to schedule your meeting.

Tips for Scheduling Meetings

◆ Ask key participants when they are available. Consider the *open house meeting* and the *staggered agenda meeting* to accommodate conflicting schedules. In an open house meeting, ask participants to stop by your office during a designated time frame to obtain or deliver written information. For a staggered agenda meeting, ask participants to be present only for the agenda item that requires their attention. Your agenda plan will help you know when to ask them to be at the meeting and for how long. Keeping to your agenda is crucial during the staggered agenda meeting.

◆ Check to find out when the room you need is available.

◆ Check your audio-visual resources if you need special equipment for your presentation, such as a videotape recorder/player and a television monitor.

◆ Check travel arrangements for participants.

Avoid scheduling meetings for Monday mornings, Friday afternoons, and the mornings after holidays.

◆ Avoid peak productivity time, such as Tuesday through Thursday mornings, unless you're scheduling a work session. Protect this time so that people can get their jobs done. Often, the hour before lunch or quitting time is productive because people avoid unnecessary delays that might otherwise extend the meeting time into their private lives.

◆ As a general rule, avoid Monday mornings, the mornings after holidays, Friday afternoons, the afternoons before holidays, and the hour after lunch. People are in transition during these times. Their bodies may be present, but their brains may be off work.

◆ If you plan periodic meetings to discuss the upcoming week, consider Thursday afternoons. People are alert then. Waiting until Monday puts you behind before you start; holding it on Friday puts you in conflict with daydreams of the weekend.

◆ Consider outside times, such as a breakfast meeting, a weekend retreat, or a brief meeting while several of you carpool or walk together.

Use the guidesheets you already have (the Four-P Needs Assessment, the Meeting Summary Chart, the Agenda Planning Worksheet, Tentative Agenda, and the Tips for Scheduling Meetings) to plan your meeting. These guidesheets, coupled with decisions regarding time and space, will give you the basis for knowing your audience and promoting the meeting.

2

Meeting Plan

WHY will we meet? (Objective, background, kind of meeting.)

WHO will attend? (Leader, presenters, participants, observers, others.)

WHAT will we do? (Objective, background, agenda items/questions.)

WHERE and WHEN will we meet? (Tentative date, day, time, duration.)

HOW MUCH will the meeting cost?

- Hourly rate of all participants and presenters: $ _____
- Rental fees for facilities and equipment: _____
- Travel expenses (if any):   _____
- Communication expenses: _____
- Materials expenses: _____
- Special accommodations, such as refreshments: _____
- My preparation time: _____
- Other: _____

ESTIMATED COST: $ _____

Chapter *Three*

Organizing the Presentation

Chapter Objectives

▶ Follow nine guidelines for effective public speaking.

▶ Master eight ways to develop a presentation topic.

> **"As a vessel is known by its sound, whether it be cracked or not; so men are proved by their speeches, whether they be wise or foolish."**
>
> ***Demosthenes***

For many people, organizing and delivering presentations may cause anxiety or outright fright. Some people say they'd rather face death than get up in front of a group and talk! Yet, getting up in front of a group and talking is part of conducting a meeting. Sometimes you can delegate the actual presentation to someone else. Or, maybe you'll be so lucky that someone volunteers.

Perhaps you've made it this far in the business world without tripping over your tongue or stumbling through your notes. If not, welcome to the club. The tips in this chapter will help you and your audience have a positive presentation.

The secret is to take one step at a time. The Nine Essential Es of Speaking and the Eight Ways to Develop a Topic will take you through the process. The image and rehearsal tips will help you polish your style. What will you gain? Increased confidence and competence! Let's begin by identifying the characteristics of effective speaking.

Nine Essential Es of Speaking

The Nine Essential Es of speaking are:

1. Build *Esteem.*

2. Arrive *Early.*

3. Be *Enthusiastic.*

4. Make *Eye* Contact.

5. Provide *Experiences.*

6. Give *Evidence.*

7. Show *Empathy.*

8. *End* on Time.

9. *Evaluate* Strengths.

Build Esteem

Good preparation and organization will increase your self-confidence. It's easier to expect success when you're ready for it. With each successful meeting, you build a reputation. Your coworkers will trust you to put together an effective and efficient meeting each time you conduct one.

A flow of words is no proof of wisdom.
Anon.

Arrive Early

Get to the meeting place 15 minutes to an hour before the meeting begins. If you're familiar with the room and you're planning a simple meeting, a few minutes is all you'll need to assess and adjust the equipment, the visual displays, the seating, the temperature, and the ventilation. If you're unfamiliar with the room or you're planning a complex meeting, allow more time for setting up.

Be Enthusiastic

Your energy and interest levels during your meeting will directly influence your audience's attention level. Know what to say, how to say it, and when to say it. If you are nervous about speaking and think it will interfere with your effectiveness, here's a secret tactic to use.

Give yourself permission to admit your fear to your audience and then commit to do your best. You might say, "I'm nervous about being in front of you today. Public speaking is a new skill I'm learning. Perhaps jumping over the Grand Canyon on a motorcycle or splitting an arrow stuck in a target would be easier. But I'm told that our company doesn't need any more motorcyclists or archers! Yet we do need risk takers. So, I'm here today to do my best for you." People respond well to such honesty. And they're glad you're in front of the group, rather than themselves.

Make Eye Contact

In some cultures, such as those of Orientals and Native Americans, it is impolite and disrespectful to look a person in the eye. However, in today's American business culture, making eye contact is a sign of good manners and respect. Audiences expect this treatment, and they resent and distrust speakers who avoid it.

Provide Experiences

Offering experiences is the fifth "E" of speaking. Three ways to do this are by telling stories, using analogies, and planning activities. The trick to making your meeting memorable is to elicit the emotions and senses of your audience. Allow members to participate through personal descriptions of events, including feelings, sights, sounds, and movement. Stories are powerful and effective tools in making your meeting positive, but remember that it's crucial that the meeting end by the agreed time. Don't let a long story sidetrack your agenda.

Give Evidence

Provide background, facts, observations, and rationale to support the purpose of your agenda. Interpret statistics fairly by stating their value as well as their limits. Make evidence as specific and concrete as possible so people can easily understand it.

> **Words are but wind, but seeing is believing.**
> *Proverb*

Show Empathy

Be considerate of your participants by keeping in mind their professional and personal needs. Give participants the information and direction they need to do their jobs as well as they can. Give them a break if attention lags.

Note: The mind can absorb only what the seat can endure!

3

End on Time

Two excuses for failing to end a meeting on time are legitimate. The first is that the group agrees to continue the meeting beyond its scheduled end in order to avoid rescheduling or to preserve the group's momentum. And the second reason is that you finish early! Announce the meeting's ending time on all communications sent to those expected to attend, and repeat it at the opening of the meeting. Avoid a dispute by agreeing at the beginning of the meeting to use a certain clock, watch, or timer to keep track of the time.

Evaluate Strengths

If you are new at conducting meetings, be positive about what you want to work on and what you want to improve. Effective change takes time. Ask yourself what you can do better next time, rather than what you do not want to do again.

The Nine Essential Es of Speaking will improve your presentation as will the following Eight Ways to Develop a Topic.

Eight Ways to Develop a Topic

You will want to answer as many of your audience's questions as possible while you're giving the presentation.

Developing a topic means writing notes or a script about what to say, how to say it, and when to say it in your presentation. You will want to answer as many of your audience's questions as possible while you're giving the presentation. This saves time in that it clarifies many uncertainties before they spawn confusion. A well-developed topic also provides a realistic picture of the objective at hand and increases the chances for creative decisions. The Eight Ways to Develop a Topic are:

1. DIRECT

2. AIDA

3. Seven Ws

4. Listing

5. Looping

6. Outlining

7. Mapping

8. Flowcharting

DIRECT

The *DIRECT* approach is a six-part system that forms an acrostic, a word in which each letter represents an idea. This approach refers to definitions, illustrations, relationships, experiences, circumstances, and testimonials. It encourages you to think about your topic in ways you may have overlooked.

◆ What *definitions* will the audience need to know to understand this topic?

◆ What *illustrations,* both visual and verbal, would help?

◆ What *relationships,* such as comparisons, causes, effects, or steps, exist?

◆ What *experiences,* such as stories, activities, or groupings, would help?

◆ What *circumstances,* such as facts, observations, or conditions, exist?

◆ What *testimonials* or quotations would influence the audience?

AIDA

AIDA is an acronym, a word created from the first letters of a series of words. It represents attention, interest, desire, and action. Advertisers and marketers use this model to design sales and promotional materials. Because you are "selling or promoting" a meeting, this model will work for you.

◆ What will get your audience's *attention?*

◆ What will hold their *interest?*

◆ What will arouse their *desire* to commit to the meeting plan?

◆ What *action* do you want and how will you get it?

The better you know your audience and your subject, the easier this is to do. If you do a good job promoting your meeting, you will have gone a long way toward getting the audience's attention and commitment. Keeping your meeting on schedule will also focus their attention. Making sure your meeting has a distinct, defined purpose will hold their interest. Getting them

If you do a good job promoting your meeting, you will have gone a long way toward getting the audience's attention and commitment.

3

all involved in discussions and decisions will build desire. Asking them for their expertise and opinions will encourage them to act. Your agenda corresponds to this model. Now use the same process for your topic.

Seven Ws

The *Seven Ws* include the five traditional questions—who, what, when, where, and why—and two more—want and wonder. You saw this approach when you worked on the agenda.

◆ *Who* needs to know about this topic, or who is involved in it?

◆ *What* is this topic, based on definition, experience, or analysis?

◆ *When* is this topic relevant, or how is it placed in history?

◆ *Where* is this topic found, or where is it important?

◆ *Why* is this topic important?

◆ What else do you *want* your audience to know?

◆ What else will your audience still *wonder* about?

Use the seven W-words shown here as headings for your topic development. Put them on a flip chart, a marker board, or a transparency for use during your presentation. You may want to combine this system with the DIRECT approach or the AIDA model. All three systems work well together.

Listing

Listing involves brainstorming ideas and points of interest about the topic, deciding which ones you'll use, and then arranging them in a logical order. The advantage of this method is that it's simple and fast. The disadvantage is that you may forget to include something important or interesting. Listing may be combined with any of the three previous ways to develop a topic. A list of key words may be all you need to serve as notes during an oral presentation and could become a handout or a visual aid. If you want more than a few key words as notes, write or type a script with wide margins and triple-spaced lines. The extra space makes your script easier to read.

> **A list of key words may be all you need to serve as notes during an oral presentation.**

3

Looping

Looping takes a list of key words that are arranged in a logical order and develops each word into a written or spoken paragraph. The first key word is linked to the second key word in the first paragraph, the second to the third in the second paragraph and so on, until the final word loops back to the first word. This illustration shows how it works.

■ *Looping* is my favorite way to begin writing a presentation because the system has a clear beginning and end, and it's fun. I enjoy watching the circular pattern evolve as I link key thoughts into a logical *development*.

The *development* of any presentation is important if the leader wants the audience to understand and to participate in decisions involving the presented material. One way to help participants follow your ideas is to provide them with clear and frequent *transitions*.

Transitions are markers, words, or phrases that tell your audience how you get from one main idea to the next or how you explain a main idea. Examples of these markers are "for example," "however," "therefore," and "finally, the third point I want to make is. . . ." Well-placed and well-defined transitions help your presentation style *flow*.

In addition, this *flow* is achieved by the repetition of one key word from the end of a paragraph to the beginning of the next paragraph. This repetition guides the participants' thinking as you present your material. It also provides a built-in system for unifying your introduction with your conclusion by eventually bringing your audience back to the first key word. No other topic development does this as well as *looping*.

Outlining

Outlining is a traditional development tool that most of us learned early in school. The worst part of outlining is thinking of two subheadings for every heading. The next awful task is getting the corresponding details lined up! Here's a hint.

Instead of this: *Do this:*

I. _____   + _____
    A. _____   • _____
    1. _____   – _____
    2. _____   • _____
    B. _____   • _____
II. _____   – _____
                        – _____

Using the graphic symbols instead of the traditional numbers and letters will free you to think about the content rather than its sequence and format. It doesn't matter whether your columns match or your Arabic numbers follow your Roman numerals. Develop your ideas by using the graphic symbols of your choice to represent each level of detail.

Mapping

Mapping shows levels of detail similar to outlining. To use mapping as a development tool, use key words and connectors within the topic diagram. An example of mapping looks similar to a family tree.

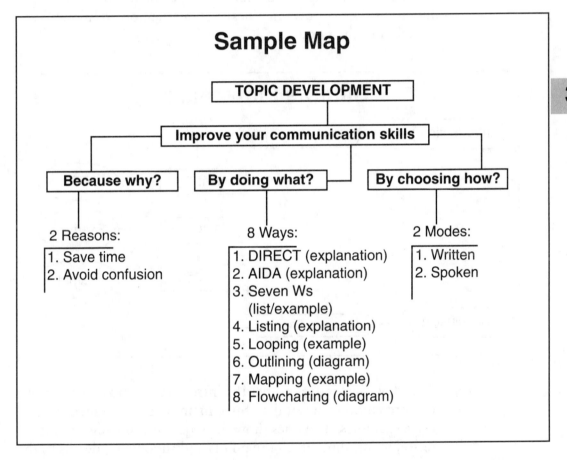

Sample Map

TOPIC DEVELOPMENT

Improve your communication skills

| Because why? | By doing what? | By choosing how? |

2 Reasons:
1. Save time
2. Avoid confusion

8 Ways:
1. DIRECT (explanation)
2. AIDA (explanation)
3. Seven Ws (list/example)
4. Listing (explanation)
5. Looping (example)
6. Outlining (diagram)
7. Mapping (example)
8. Flowcharting (diagram)

2 Modes:
1. Written
2. Spoken

Flowcharting

The eighth way to develop a topic is *flowcharting*. For each function of the information given, use a different shape in a diagram. Use a rectangle, for instance, to represent a main point, use an oval for a definition, a circle for an example, a triangle for a cause, or any shapes you choose for specific information functions. Use connecting lines to show the flow from one function to the next.

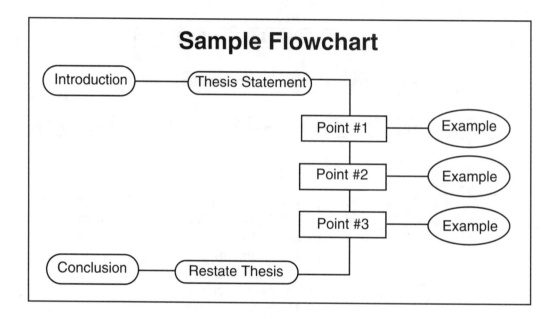

This flowchart indicates that the introduction and conclusion in this presentation are similar, three main points are stated, and three examples. The lines show the sequence, moving from the introduction through all the points and supporting details to the conclusion.

Whether you prefer notes or diagrams, you must find several ways to develop your topic. If you hit a writer's block, simply use one of these methods to get unblocked. For example, a progress report or a proposal may be presented best as a chronological flowchart that moves through background information to the current situation and into recommendations for the future. The DIRECT approach offers a variety of information, and the AIDA model focuses on the audience's perception. Each method will help provide a clear, concise, and convincing presentation.

Chapter *Four*

Rehearsing the Presentation

Chapter Objectives

▶ Project a positive visual image and vocal image when speaking.

▶ Follow 12 tips for rehearsing your presentation.

Having a well-prepared presentation will increase your confidence. Part of preparation is composing and organizing the material you must cover in the meeting. Another part of preparation is composing and organizing yourself! This chapter offers tips for presenting your visual and vocal image. Then you'll see how these images interact as you use the rehearsal tips.

> **How you present yourself is as important as how you present your topic.**

How you present yourself is as important as how you present your topic. Your visual image projects a message even before your voice does. One favorite social-behavior study tested the public's bias toward well-groomed, attractive people. In the study, several men and women appear well groomed and attractive in some photographs, and frumpy, severe, and unattractive in others. The public perceived the attractive people as more competent and confident than the unattractive people, not realizing the photographs were of the same people. Some people said they'd give the well-groomed people higher salaries and more chances to overcome failures. In almost all instances, well-groomed, attractive people have the advantage. So take the time to look good!

Your vocal image is as important as your visual image. If your vocal characteristics are unpleasant—monotone, shrill, or nasal—people will hear only the sound of your voice, not your words. If your speech is too loud, too soft, too fast, or too slow, people will quit listening. If your audience has to work at understanding your words, they'll give up and let you talk to yourself. Some tips follow.

Visual Image Tips

◆ As you prepare to talk, people will focus on your face. Check your hair, makeup, collar and shoulders for any distractions such as labels, smudges, and lint.

◆ Avoid jewelry, ties, or other accessories that draw attention. You'll want the audience's attention on what you're saying rather than on what you're wearing.

◆ Wear solid colors, subtle plaids, or small-scaled prints in predominantly neutral and cool shades, such as grays and blues. These calm colors will help you look and feel in control. Large prints can distract and appear to add weight. Wear comfortable, stylish clothing that allows you to move, yet fits smoothly.

◆ Nothing hurts worse than shoes that are uncomfortable. Choose your shoes for the meeting based on comfort as well as appearance.

◆ If you are short, stand on a riser. Stand behind a lectern only if you're on a step stool. If you are tall, you may want to sit on a stool so that your face is at a comfortable height for the seated audience members to see.

◆ Your posture is a direct gauge of your command over an audience. When you stand and sit straight, your audience assumes you are confident with your presentation.

◆ Smile occasionally and appropriately. Smiling all the time is not natural. Generally, it's best to smile after the introductions when you're meeting someone for the first time. People take you more seriously after knowing your name.

◆ Consult with a professional image counselor for more ideas that are specific to you.

4

Vocal Image Tips

♦ Tape yourself having a conversation with a friend. Listen for speech mannerisms, such as fillers, inflections, and rate. "Um" and "OK" repeated 26 times in 60 seconds is irritating. You may not hear these repetitions until you listen to a tape!

♦ Drink water before and during vocal exercise to keep your throat lubricated. Avoid carbonated or alcoholic beverages to prevent burping and slurring.

Lower your pitch to appear calm and in command.

♦ Lower your pitch to appear calm and in command. While listening to the radio on the way to work this week, practice singing along in a lower octave. Another way to be in command is to use short, assertive statements, such as "I need your help now" or "We need a decision now."

♦ Breathe from your abdomen in slow, deep breaths. This relaxes your upper body to allow a rich sound that projects easily. Also, open the back of your throat when you talk. You can feel this when you open your mouth and tilt your chin upward. Again, this helps you project your voice.

♦ Practice the sounds of your enthusiasm. A vivid, vivacious voice is impossible to ignore.

♦ Practice pronouncing the total word. Lazy speech suggests a lazy mind or at least a tired mouth. Don't say gonna for going, sketti for spaghetti, and coulda for could have.

♦ Consult a speech therapist or an experienced speaker for more ideas.

Rehearsal Tips

♦ Write out key words or a script for your presentation.

♦ Read or recite it silently before going further.

♦ Drink approximately one-half glass of water to lubricate your throat and voice before speaking. Drink the other half of your water as you read or recite your presentation aloud. If your speech is short, you may not need the extra water. But it's smart to have it ready just in case. Also, by needing water, your body will tell you when you've been talking too long without a break!

♦ Summarize your main points aloud as if responding to a question.

♦ Define key terms aloud as if your audience has asked for them.

♦ Tape your speaking part. Time it. Shorten or expand it.

♦ Listen to the audiotape. Determine what you'll change. Listen for proper pace, volume, and pauses.

♦ Assemble a friendly, small audience if possible.

♦ Give your entire presentation with visuals and equipment. Use the microphone and videotape recorder if they're part of your presentation. Practice the best walking and positioning patterns for yourself so you'll miss tripping over cords. Tape cords to the floor. Speak to all of the empty seats. Practice your eye contact and eye movement around the room. Videotape this practice if possible.

♦ Watch your tape. Refine sections by practicing in front of a mirror.

♦ Affirm your strengths. Give yourself compliments and encouragement.

♦ Visualize yourself having successfully delivered the presentation. Bask in this feeling so you'll know how to reconstruct it during the real event!

Write out key words or a script for your presentation.

4

43

The preparation phase of your presentation will make or break your meeting. To monitor your thoroughness, use this checklist of details. Your hard work during this phase will pay off!

Preparation Checklist

Meeting Date:_____ Objective:_____

Task	Completed/Not Necessary	
	(X)	(N/A)
Take *Self-Assessment Survey*	_____	
Use *Four-P Needs Assessment*	_____	
Prepare *Tentative Agenda*	_____	
Complete *Meeting Plan*	_____	
Develop presentation	_____	
Review image tips	_____	
Rehearse presentation	_____	
Complete *Completion Checklist* (page 88)	_____	

Chapter *Five*

Arranging the Room

Chapter Objective

▶ Choose an appropriate seating arrangement for your meeting.

When two or more people agree to meet at a certain place at a specific time to interact in some way, a meeting results. Technology has expanded our ability to meet in unusual places at unusual times. Teleconferences, video conferences, and computer-network conferences allow us to meet across town, country, or globe without physically traveling outside our offices. Yet we conduct most of our business through the traditional face-to-face meeting by gathering in the same room at the same hour. Understanding the characteristics of groups and interactions within groups will help you conduct effective meetings by achieving synergy rather than wasting energy.

Characteristics of Groups

Two basic characteristics of groups are crucial for you to know:

The primary function of the meeting influences seating choices.

♦ The size of the group influences your meeting management.

♦ The primary function of the meeting influences seating choices.

Here's how your group's size and primary function will affect your meeting:

◆ Size will determine how you label the group:

pair or dyad	=	2 members
triad	=	3 members
small group	=	4 to 15 members
medium group	=	16 to 25 members
large group	=	26 to 99 members
huge group	=	100 or more members

◆ Size also determines what you can expect from a group. The small group offers more options for a meeting place and time, quicker decisions from participants, less structure, more personal and informal discussion, more movement-oriented interaction, and more cooperation from the group. The odd-numbered small group, usually composed of three to nine members, is best for making fast decisions. Five to 11 members are good for resolving problems. A small group is easier to arrange in a circle, making each member visible and audible to the entire group. Participation is usually high in a small group.

◆ The larger the group, the more competitive subgroups are within the group. As the number of participants increases in your meeting, consider asking members to help as recorder, reporter, or timekeeper. Consider coleaders for subgroups within the large group. Each subgroup then acts similar to a small group.

The larger the group, the more competitive subgroups are within the group.

◆ People sit closer together when they meet in a large room and have a positive perception of the leader. Most Americans sit within three feet of another person and stand an average of 18 inches apart. The more motivated people are in a group, the closer they sit together and the more often they say "we" instead of "I." But if they sit together too closely too quickly, before they've built rapport and trust, their attitudes tend to be negative.

◆ People sit farther apart if they are independent, unmotivated, disinterested, or feeling negative or competitive. Those who are subordinates or superiors to the other group members will also sit farther apart than they would with their peers.

♦ Some members of a group, no matter the size, will claim a spot in the meeting room and won't move without resistance. If a member prefers one particular seat, she or he may be resentful of intruders in the area. People who wear beepers may purposefully and thoughtfully claim a seat close to an exit to minimize the group's distraction. Others may sit where they can hear and see well. You may have to accommodate these claims when you shift among exercises in a meeting.

Where and with whom people sit in a meeting influences their participation and your preparation. As the physical and psychological distances among members of a group decrease, motivation and interaction increase. Distances among members vary with time, combinations of people, and the task. Your job is to monitor the distances!

Seating Arrangements

Being aware of the location of doors, windows, aisles, visual displays, and comfort centers, such as telephones, restrooms, and refreshments will help you determine the best seating arrangement for your group. The seven most common arrangements are the conference, U-shape, circle, pod, classroom, chevron, and theater styles. Each of these is diagrammed on the following pages.

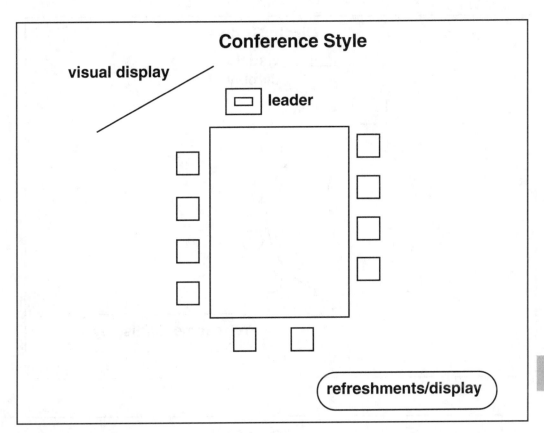

Conference Style

visual display

leader

refreshments/display

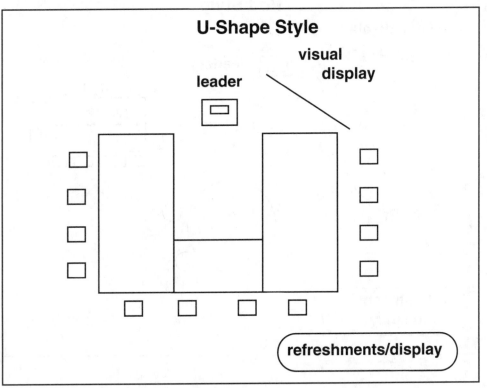

U-Shape Style

visual display

leader

refreshments/display

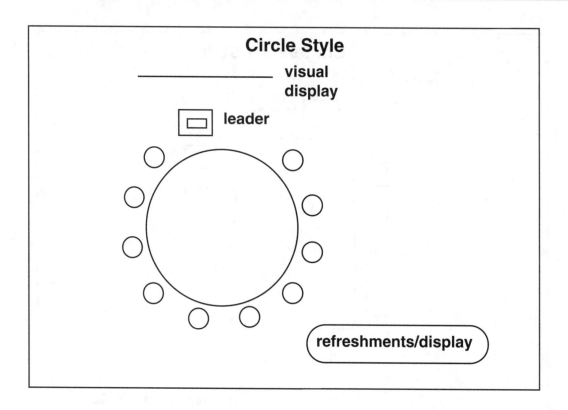

Circle Style

_____ visual display

leader

refreshments/display

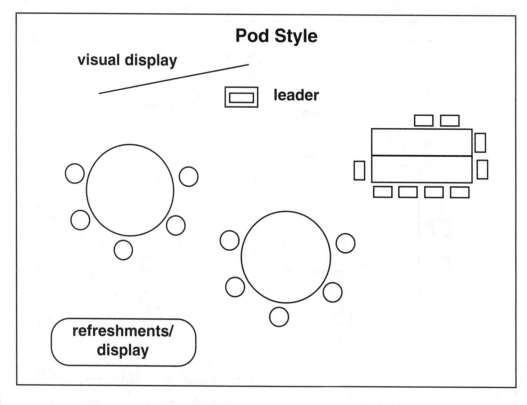

Pod Style

visual display

leader

refreshments/ display

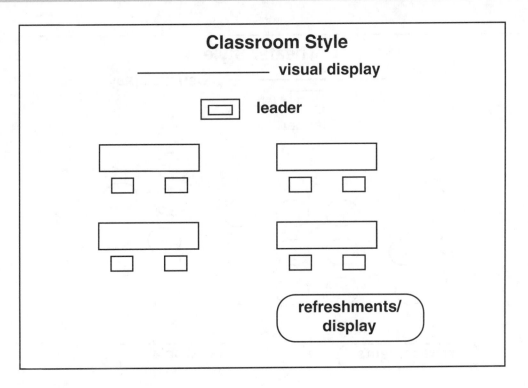

Classroom Style

—————————— visual display

leader

refreshments/
display

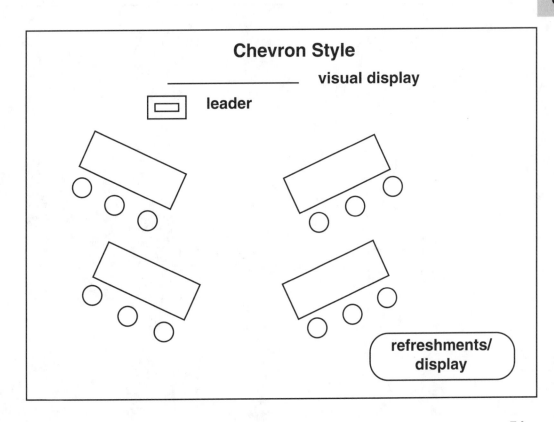

Chevron Style

—————————— visual display

leader

refreshments/
display

5

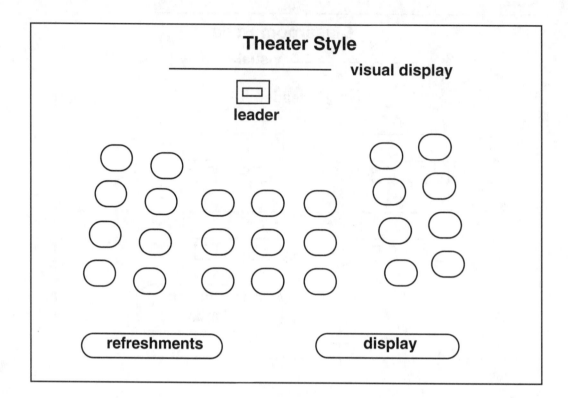

The chart below will help you determine which arrangement to use for your meeting if you have some flexibility.

Seating Arrangement Chart

Style	Room Size	Group Size	Primary Function
Conference	Small	Small	Inform/ perform/ form
U-Shape	Small/medium	Small	Inform/ form
Circle	Small/medium	Small/ medium	Inform/ form/ conform
Pod	Medium	Medium+	Form/ perform
Classroom	Medium	Large	Inform/ conform
Chevron	Medium+	Large	Inform/ conform
Theater	Large	Large	Inform/ conform

5

Choosing Your Arrangement

Each of these arrangements has its advantages and disadvantages. For example, if your room is small, you can accommodate the conference, U-shape, or circle styles for a group of four to 16 members. If the room is larger with portable chairs and tables, you have the most flexibility of style. If you're planning a work session, consider the pod and conference styles. The pod style, however, is less comfortable and requires some movement of chairs for members to see any visuals or the speaker well. If tables are needed for writing during the meeting, avoid the theater and circle styles. The chevron style is a variation of the classroom style. It staggers the members into diagonal rather than vertical rows to allow an unobstructed view of and from the podium.

> **However the room is arranged, the speaker will want to be able to walk within a few feet of all the members.**

Having a center aisle or two inside aisles allows convenient pathways in the classroom, chevron, and theater styles for the speaker to move close to all members of the group. If the group is arranged in short rows, the two outside aisles may be enough. However the room is arranged, the speaker will want to be able to walk within a few feet of all the members. This allows everyone to hear and respond better.

Be thoughtful about any special needs of participants. These include ramps and wider aisles for wheelchairs, walkers, and canes; front seating or an extra place next to the speaker for an interpreter for the hearing impaired; and back or aisle seating for those who must respond quickly to beepers and emergency calls. Consider your room arrangement carefully. The size of the room and the size and special needs of the group will impact the function and success of your meeting.

Chapter *Six*

Managing the Group

Chapter Objectives

▶ Deal with conflict that can arise during a meeting.

▶ Use team leadership skills to deal with group dynamics during a meeting.

▶ Improve group listening skills.

> To manage men, one ought to have a sharp mind in a velvet sheath.
> *George Eliot*

Meetings come in all sizes, from one to 100. No matter what the size, meetings usually involve the need for those in attendance to interact together and make decisions. As group leader, it is your job to manage and facilitate this process within the meeting group and help participants reach the most effective decisions possible.

Three types of skills will help you use involvement and commitment to achieve your meeting's goals:

◆ Conflict resolution skills

◆ Team leadership skills

◆ Listening skills

Managing Conflict

Most conflict results from differences in experiences and expectations. Conflict gives us the opportunity to recognize other viewpoints and challenges us to be more creative in our thinking than we would otherwise. A meeting without conflict will end quickly with an acceptable result; a meeting with conflict may end later with a potentially better result.

Creative, constructive conflict builds both confidence and competence. Destructive conflict leads to uncooperative, argumentative, and, perhaps, aggressive coworkers—a situation that compounds frustration and fear.

Seven Cs for Resolving Conflict

Conflict-resolution skills are essential for an effective leader in any meeting. The following chart shows the Seven Cs, the common behavioral styles for resolving conflict. Knowing the characteristics of these styles will help you determine what's most appropriate for directing your meeting and your audience.

Seven Cs for Resolving Conflict

Method:	Conceal	Control	Compete	Compromise	Coact	Collaborate	Concur
Approach:	individual		group			team	
Demeanor:	(passive)	(assertive/ aggressive)	(assertive/ aggressive)	(passive/ assertive)	(passive/ aggressive)	(assertive)	(assertive)
Emphasis:	Conflict ·· Consensus						

6

◆ **Conceal**
   To *conceal* means to deny a conflict or problem, ignore it, or hope it will go away. Sometimes a miracle happens to change the situation so that you no longer have to deal with it, but usually this only postpones and intensifies the inevitable confrontation. Concealing is not an effective way to deal with conflict. Passive behavior often leads to unsatisfied needs and unsatisfactory results, allowing the conflict to remain without resolution.

◆ **Control**
   To *control* means that the individual takes charge of the decision-making process either by consulting with others or dictating to them. This approach is most effective in managing a crisis, a severe time constraint, or a routine decision, but least effective in managing almost any other kind of situation.

In any argument, the man with the greater intelligence is always wrong, because he did not use his intelligence to avoid the argument in the first place.
Anon.

At the midpoint of the continuum, more than one person makes the decision or chooses the resolution.

◆ **Compete**
To *compete* means that one group or coalition may achieve a goal while another group or coalition cannot. This is a desirable method only if you're on the winning side!

◆ **Compromise**
To *compromise* means concessions or trades will get you part of what you want. This will happen if the goals are not mutual or if the methods used by the negotiating parties vary greatly. A mediator or an arbitrator will assist the group in reaching an understanding. The compromise is the middle ground between conflict (no agreement) and consensus (total agreement).

> **A group who agrees on a goal and how to accomplish it acts as a team.**

◆ **Coact**
To coact means to cooperate but without complete cooperation. The goals may be mutual, but the expectations and experiences of the group are not shared. This method will benefit many members. To compete, to compromise, and to coact are group approaches to decision making and problem solving.

A group who agrees on a goal and how to accomplish it acts as a team. Team approaches to resolving conflict are the most enduring because they benefit the most members.

◆ **Collaborate**
To *collaborate* means to work together in harmony to reach a decision. Many leaders appear during the meeting's discussion. Everyone agrees to support the final decision, although some may still have reservations.

◆ **Concur**
To *concur* means that everyone agrees to the final decision without reservation. No peer pressure or lazy thinking causes this agreement. Each member of the team must be committed to the goal and to the team. Each member acts as your coleader, who participates and communicates actively. Through conflict and chaos, a group becomes a team with a consensus.

Managing Conflict One-on-One

You may often find yourself meeing with just one person to set individual performance and development goals, resolve a problem or eliminate an obstacle, develop a relationship, or complete a plan of action.

Begin any one-on-one meeting by choosing a location that is convenient and acceptable to both of you. You may need a place that is private if the nature of your meeting is to discuss individual performance. Perhaps meeting in one of your offices or at a restaurant would provide the appropriate environment. If the purpose of your meeting is comfortable for both of you, you may stand or sit. If your meeting is uncomfortable for one or both of you, sit together at the corner or along the side of a table. Avoid sitting across a table or desk from each other because that puts you in an adversarial position. Unlikely partners have worked together, including East and West Germany, America, and Russia, and Apple Computer and IBM. If these larger concerns were able to come together, then surely it is possible to negotiate a smaller concern with Jerry or Chris!

> **Begin any one-on-one meeting by choosing a location that is convenient and acceptable to both of you.**

The SEES Confrontation Model provides an effective strategy for dealing with conflict during a one-on-one meeting:
S   Signal
E   Explanation
E   Example
S   Significance

6

◆ **Signal your concern.**
1. Use positive verbal and nonverbal language. Keep your posture open with your arms and legs uncrossed. This is a persuasive posture. For example, say, "Thank you for meeting with me. Working together, we can make this situation productive."

2. Ask for commitment. "Will you work with me to resolve this situation?"

◆ **Explain the situation.**
1. Ask your partner to identify the problem or conflict. "How do you understand the situation?"

2. Listen without interruption.

3. Restate or paraphrase your partner's explanation until your partner says you understand it correctly. "Do I understand correctly? You said. . . ."

♦ **Describe a specific, current example of the situation.**
   • Clarify your view of this situation. Keep your view based on observation, and avoid judgment or assumption. Make sure that your facts and interpretations are accurate and fair. Find something in your partner's statement to agree with. "I agree that . . . and I see . . . differently . . . For example . . . "

♦ **Conclude with the significance of the resolution.**
   1. State your expectations, the consequences, and the effects.

   2. Ask for agreement on the goal and its criteria. Who does what by when? If the process needs to be determined by both of you, discuss how it will happen. This agreement should be specific and realistic, positive and productive, measurable and dated.

   3. Summarize the meeting and end positively and supportively. "Thank you for your time and help. Your ideas will bring success. We'll meet next Tuesday at 10 a.m. in your office to review our action plan."

The SEES Confrontation Model is a general strategy you can modify for any one-to-one meeting.

The SEES Confrontation Model is a general strategy you can modify for any one-to-one meeting. Frustrations and fears are the major causes of failed meetings and result from needs that are not satisfied. Identifying the obstacles and working together to remove them and to empower one another will prevent, reduce, or eliminate frustration or fear. People avoid confrontation because they fear losing someone's favor, losing their own temper, losing their anger, or losing their indispensability. With every change, there's some distress. Yet stress can paralyze or energize us.

Team Leadership Skills

The following are ways to focus your team during meetings to concentrate on the process and the objective rather than on the individual personalities:

♦ **Stay connected.**
Communicate with each member and encourage all members to communicate directly with others. Stay in touch with dissenters and work toward resolution. Build a network.

♦ **Restate expectations.**
Repeat and clarify what you will do, what you won't do, what you believe, and what you think. Keep your values and priorities well defined.

♦ **Be detached.**
This sounds like a paradox, and it is! You will communicate better if you can distance yourself from any disagreement. Respond calmly. You may not like or understand a member's comment, but you may have to accept or acknowledge it. Keep an open mind.

> Communicate with each member and encourage all members to communicate directly with others.

The Law of Combinations, a systemic approach to group behavior, shows that relationships are powerful connections. For example, Sandy may be independent alone, dependent with Marge, belligerent with Nate, and empowering with Mark. Sandy has the same personality, yet the connections differ. Sandy's interaction with each individual's personality traits causes a different reaction from Sandy. You see this in meetings all the time. Someone who usually works hard on one team slacks off when moved to another group. An overachiever in one place connects with an underachiever somewhere else.

The Law of Combinations explains why group dynamics change so often: as the combinations of people change, the relationships change. The group has a complex personality of its own. When the balance in that system changes, the meeting leader will experience resistance! Keeping balance within a meeting so that the group can become a team means paying attention to the combinations and communications.

6

An effective meeting facilitator knows a variety of strategies for encouraging members to participate and communicate, redirecting participation and communication when it's necessary. If something should interrupt the flow of your meeting, follow the three strategy lists for preventing and reducing these unproductive situations: Tips to Improve Listening, Tips to Increase Involvement, and Tips to Transform Disagreement.

Developing Listening Skills

Few of us know how to say nothing. Few of us know when.

Anon.

Listening is a fundamental communication skill, yet it is the most difficult skill to do well. Conducting a well-prepared meeting won't do you any good if the participants aren't listening to you or each other, or if you aren't listening to them! Everyone's attention will improve as listening improves. Use these tips to become a better listener. Then use these tips again to become a better speaker and leader in your meetings! Good listening saves both time and effort.

Tips to Improve Individual Listening

◆ Listen with your best ear. Most people hear more effectively and efficiently through their left ears. Which ear do you use most often while talking on the telephone? Turn that ear toward your audience.

◆ Be actively silent. Speak only to clarify or summarize. Place a hand over your mouth if you have to!

◆ Identify assumptions you are making and avoid mind reading. Once a man saw another man moving a piano into a store. He offered to help. They pushed till they were exhausted. The store owner gasped, "I can't believe this piano is so difficult to get out of here." The stranger said, "Out? Oh, no!"

Identify assumptions you are making and avoid mind reading.

◆ Listen for the person's transitions, such as "Another important point is . . ." "For example . . ." "To further explain . . ."

◆ Use visualization techniques to imagine what the speaker says. Create a mental movie of the message.

6

◆ Connect new ideas to information you already know, such as "I can apply these tips for listening better to talking on the phone with clients."

◆ Restate what the person just said before making your own comment.

◆ Tell yourself to learn something new from this person.

Tips to Improve Group Listening

♦ Place yourself next to your listener's left side during a conversation or a presentation.

♦ Ask your listeners for their attention.

♦ Provide an overview or outline for your audience to follow.

Provide an overview or outline for your audience to follow.

♦ Tell your listeners how they'll benefit from the meeting, such as "This information will save you time."

♦ Use clear, concrete transitions.

♦ Whisper. Vary the volume of your voice.

♦ Speed up or slow down. Vary the pace of your speech.

♦ Stop talking.

♦ Ask those who can hear you to do something, such as "If you can hear me, stomp your foot," or "Say 'yes' twice." Other members will quiet down to find out what's going on!

♦ Give the group a break.

♦ Make or do something unusual, yet relevant to your point.

♦ Promise to keep the meeting short, and then keep your promise.

♦ Smile or laugh, then relate something humorous to make your point.

♦ Move to keep your audience focused. Point to visuals, walk toward talkers and use wide gestures to maintain attention.

♦ Eliminate outside distractions, such as phones ringing and beepers sounding in the meeting room.

♦ Provide a comfortable temperature and straight-backed chairs for your audience.

♦ Increase your audience's involvement in the meeting.

Increasing Involvement

Before you can get people involved in making decisions and setting action plans in your meeting, you must get them to listen. However, some may be unmotivated still. Your meeting goes nowhere without their participation and commitment. Once participants become part of the process for achieving the meeting's objective, the meeting will run smoothly and quickly. Here are some ideas to get you and your group started.

Tips to Increase Involvement

◆ Ask the group to identify its needs. Have group representatives record them on a display, such as a cork board, marker board, or flip chart.

◆ Ask your audience to do something with the information they have, such as "Check two items on this list that you think are top priorities."

◆ Tell a story. People get involved in stories, especially if you ask them to imagine themselves in the situation you describe. "Imagine you are just beginning this job. It's your first day here, and . . ." Each member of the audience then becomes the lead character in your story. Remember that your story should illustrate a point that is pertinent to the meeting's objective.

◆ Encourage the group to share leadership. Ask for a volunteer to lead the small group discussion. That leader then asks someone else to lead the work session.

◆ Call someone by name and invite that person to comment. Plan this by inserting a signal in your presentation notes to ask Alice or Zack about this topic or point. Ask someone who has not commented yet to offer an opinion.

◆ Ask someone to summarize what has happened in the meeting so far.

◆ Invite participants to give options rather than advice. "Have you thought of . . . " works better than "I think you ought to . . ."

> Once participants become part of the process for achieving the meeting's objective, the meeting will run smoothly and quickly.

6

65

♦ Ask members of small groups to stand along a wall or beside their chairs when they complete a task. This allows members to move and encourages them to finish the task quickly.

♦ Build in reflection time. Pause with soft music playing in the background while participants record their thoughts. The music discourages talking and encourages thinking.

♦ Recognize emotions and body language. If Tony's head shakes, say, "Tony, you're shaking your head. Would you share what you're thinking with us?"

Ask whether the group has any questions, concerns, or suggestions.

♦ Ask whether the group has any questions, concerns, or suggestions.

♦ Ask the group to determine the best action plan, including specific tasks, people responsible for the completion of tasks, and the time frame for the tasks.

♦ Focus on mutual gain so that everyone feels like a winner. Find a way to demonstrate how your audience will gain from each meeting you lead.

Resolving Disagreement

Differences of opinion, misunderstandings, and mismatched priorities can cause friction any time people come together to talk. A good meeting leader will be firm, direct, and flexible in the face of conflict. Your confident manner and a strong HIDDEN Agenda will lead participants toward the consensus side of the conflict-resolution continuum.

Tips to Transform Disagreement

◆ Use humor to defuse tension. The capacity to be playful gives you the psychological distance you need to remain calm and responsive without being reactive during meetings. A spontaneous laugh can offer the fresh perspective your group needs.

◆ Find a way to agree. Find something in the other argument or comment that you can agree with at least partially. "I agree that this is an unfortunate situation, and I would remedy it differently than you have described."

Find something in the other argument or comment that you can agree with at least partially.

◆ Use *and* instead of *but*. "We lowered our cost per unit by 3 percent, and we must lower it another 4 percent by July 1." Note that using *but* in that sentence would have discounted the original accomplishment.

6

◆ If someone from the audience verbally attacks you, thank that person for the comment or the concern, break eye contact and either proceed to your next point or ask the audience to respond. Avoid getting into a shouting match or a verbal duel. Even if you win the argument, you lose your audience's confidence that you can lead the group objectively.

◆ When telling bad news, use *I* or *we* as if you "own" it. When telling good news, say *you* as if they "own" it.

◆ Use peer pressure to keep divergent comments to a minimum. Ask the group early in the discussion to remind one another to stay on the topic. Identify a signal that members can use to suggest the speaker get back to the point at hand.

♦ Ask the group to verify any gossip or interpretations that appear in the meeting in order to avoid perpetuating rumors or assumptions. "How do you know that?"

♦ Avoid triangling, complaining about a person who is not part of the conversation. This tactic leads to misunderstandings, secrets, and mistrust every time! Speak directly to a person if you want a conflict resolved.

Speak directly to a person if you want a conflict resolved.

♦ Restate a person's disagreement, and ask if you understand it correctly. Be sure you hear what that person is saying and that the person feels you are taking the disagreement seriously.

♦ Ask the person who disagrees if she or he wants it stated in the record of the meeting, or ask if the point is appropriate for the next meeting's agenda. Delaying or rescheduling such points will often defuse them. With time between this meeting and the next, some of the points will resolve themselves.

♦ If a person who is hostile toward you or the group must be in the meeting, seat that person to your side—the amicable position—and not across from you—the antagonistic position.

♦ Focus on current issues—the here and the now. You can't change the past; you can change how you respond to the present and to the future.

♦ Focus on the behavior and the issue, not the person. If someone calls you "incompetent," reply, "I hear your frustration that this matter is not resolved yet. Work with me, and together we'll find a solution."

♦ Use a mediator or an arbitrator. Ask the dissenting parties to agree to abide by the outcome that will be facilitated or decided by a person they mutually appoint.

◆ Describe observations in nonthreatening, nonjudgmental language. "You claim that . . . " suggests that the person is lying. A more neutral response is, "Is my understanding correct? Are you saying that . . . ?" Saying "Your department never gets its annual report on time" may be unfair. Perhaps the printer delayed the department's publication two of the last five years. Avoid making conclusions while describing situations.

Describe observations in nonthreatening, nonjudgmental language.

◆ Use an "I Message." This is a direct, clear, and non-threatening statement that allows the speaker to describe personal feelings, observations, and perceptions in a specific situation. Four parts of this message work together to form a complete communication about a current situation: observation, emotion, impact, and action.

■ "When I receive a report late (observation), I feel flustered (emotion). Then I don't have the time to do as good a job as I'd like to and as my supervisor would like me to do (impact). Please make a realistic deadline for your staff so that we can all count on the scheduled completion of an excellent project (action)."

The "I Message" says, "This is how I understand the situation, how I feel about it, what happens, and what I want you or me to do to keep it from happening again."

6

◆ Use the FOCUS model to transform complaints that are not negotiable into targets that are. Individuals or teams can use this process:

What are your *feelings* about the situation?	I feel . . .
What are your *objections* or concerns?	I am frustrated that . . .
What are the *consequences?*	I worry that . . .
What would *utopia* be?	I wish . . .
What *satisfaction* are you looking for?	I want . . .

69

Chapter *Seven*

Opening and Conducting the Meeting

Chapter Objectives

▶ Reduce anxiety before a meeting.

▶ Build credibility as a speaker.

▶ Introduce other speakers.

▶ Document the meeting.

Many events in life cause stress, involve risk, and offer the chance of something better. Typically, the hardest or scariest part of anything is the beginning. Each beginning signals a change—a step toward a potential transformation. Each meeting provides opportunities for each participant to become better in some way.

> My way is to begin with the beginning.
> *Don Juan*

Not everyone welcomes this chance. You, however, are in a unique position to ease the anxiety felt just before a meeting begins and during its first few minutes. Your leadership will set the tone for the meeting. You have already gone a long way toward making the meeting a valuable experience for everyone by preparing the content—including objectives, materials, and participants—and part of the context—including group dynamics, seating arrangements, and special considerations for those participants with physical or schedule constraints. Yet, before you can effectively direct a meeting, you must host the members. Hosting means further developing the context of the meeting during the greeting and the opening.

You can expect the initial minutes of the gathering to include greeting participants as they arrive and the three elements of the opening:

◆ Introductions of key presenters

◆ Acceptance of the purpose and the schedule

◆ Instructions or recommendations for direction

How can you make yourself and others more comfortable as you ease into the content of the meeting? Suggestions follow.

Reducing Your Anxiety

Present yourself as well as the content of a meeting. Realizing that others are making judgments about you and the presentation may make you nervous. Perhaps speaking in front of a group makes you even more nervous. Here are some tips to help you compose yourself, so you'll think and speak clearly.

◆ **Preparation**
Do as much as you can before the meeting day to get ready. Use the checklists in this book to keep yourself organized. Review the material an hour before the meeting and then relax. Trust your preparation.

◆ **Breathing**
Relax with a few deep breaths before you begin greeting people. Pause during a conversation or a presentation just long enough to talk yourself into being calm, collected, and clear. Breathe to a count of 10: "1, 2, 3, 4" as you inhale, and "5, 6, 7, 8, 9, 10" as you silently exhale.

◆ **Affirmations**
Write down your strengths and positive expectations for your performance during the meeting. Say these aloud. Avoid any negative thoughts. Restate your affirmations with commitment, conviction, and confidence. Decide to be successful!

> Worry affects circulation, the heart and the glands, the whole nervous system, and profoundly affects the heart. I have never known a man who died from overwork, but many who died from doubt.
>
> *Dr. Charles Mayo*

7

◆ **Visuals**
Use visuals, such as transparencies or flip charts, as presentation cues for yourself as well as aids for your audience. Once in sequence, these materials provide an outline of your content to help you keep on track and on time. You may want to make notes for yourself, too. Use a sticky note that you can quickly read and peel off a transparency as a reminder to ask a question, clarify a term, or pause for effect. Use lightly penciled notes that only you can see and read on a flip chart prepared for the audience.

◆ **Movement**
Use your body to communicate. Use your face, arms, and legs; smile, gesture, and walk. The exercise will relax you by giving your nervous energy a productive outlet.

Use your body to communicate.

◆ **Delegation**
Invite others to develop their leadership skills along with you by doing as much of the preparation and presentation as possible. Ask someone else to give a report, facilitate a work group, or photocopy materials. You have to coordinate this process, but you don't have to do it all by yourself!

◆ **Discussion**
Rely on discussion when someone asks a question you don't have an answer for or when someone says something hostile to you. Open the response to your audience, either an individual or the whole group. You may say, "I'm not sure how to respond to that. Perhaps some of you (extend your arm toward the audience) have helpful comments."

◆ **Visualization**
Visualize what a good meeting looks like and place yourself in it. Review the elements of the meeting and what you plan to say and do during each. See yourself looking attractive, sounding articulate, moving with poise, and feeling good!

You'll want to clarify your expectations and ready your audience for active listening and enthusiastic involvement during the meeting. An anxious audience has its guard up and its mind closed. To increase collaboration in achieving the meeting's objective, identify your audience's concerns.

Reducing Your Audience's Anxiety

◆ **Preparation**
Your audience will appreciate having everything in position and ready to go. It shows that you value their time. Besides, they base their perception of your competence on your preparation.

◆ **Greetings**
Meet participants at the door as they arrive. Address each by name if possible, or introduce yourself. If there are too many new people for you to remember everyone's name, ask the participants to wear name tags. Offer a positive, sincere comment, such as "Thank you for being here today" or "Did you enjoy your vacation on the coast?" to recognize each person. Learn names to gain positive attitudes.

◆ **Promise**
Make a promise to keep on the accepted schedule and topics. Everyone will appreciate your commitment to finish the agenda within the agreed time frame.

◆ **Humor**
Project a pertinent cartoon or a brief story on the wall for your audience to see when they arrive for the meeting. This will entertain them, give them a discussion piece, and encourage them to arrive early next time because they realize you reward their efforts to be on time.

◆ **Music**
Play soft, instrumental music to encourage participants to relax prior to the meeting or to internalize information and reflect on applications for new knowledge during the meeting. Music facilitates creative problem solving and is a great transitional activity between the "outside world" and the "meeting world" or between information and formation segments of the same meeting. It adds a positive dynamic to the mood of a meeting.

Make a promise to keep on the accepted schedule and topics.

7

◆ **Sharing**
Recognize the sacrifices people have made to attend the meeting. Some may have worries that will interfere with their attention during the meeting. Share updates about participants' lives, concerns, and pleasures at the start of the meeting to build personal relationships. Some meeting leaders list this time of "comfort and caring," or "sharing and caring" as the first item on their agendas.

◆ **Movement**
Encourage participants to move around during a networking time or an opening activity. Ideas for how to do this will come later in the chapter. You'll want to get everyone's minds and bodies working toward more complete commitment to the agenda. The physical activity will activate the mental activity. Exercise activates imagination!

◆ **Stories**
All great meetings include an anecdote, a simulation, or an illustration to make a point. The laughter or other emotional responses break down attention barriers that people carry into meetings. People bond with stories, and bonding reduces anxiety.

Opening a Meeting

The opening of a meeting is the opening of minds.

The opening of a meeting is the opening of minds. Consequently, how you begin a meeting is the most important part of your strategy. What a person says may not be as important as how it is said. The emphasis on certain words or certain meanings can change the message of a statement. Practice emphasizing the following underlined words:

◆ *You* will improve,

◆ You *will* improve

◆ You will *improve*.

All send different messages. To help you set the stage for a successful meeting and to build a sense of community among the participants, use any of the following ideas or allow them to spark other possibilities.

◆ Begin with an inspirational quotation, a stimulating testimonial, or a startling statistic to create interest.

◆ Use your company's values or action priorities, label signs with key words that represent them. Post them on the walls in separate locations around the room, and invite participants to take a stand under the one they think is most important now.

◆ Have participants identify topics that need discussion. Write them on sticky notes and post them in an appropriate column on a flip chart. Columns can be labeled yes/no, now/later, 1-2-3, or some other way.

◆ Display a timeline or other overview of the current project.

◆ Compare your perception with the participants' perceptions of how they will gain from this meeting.

◆ Use props, music, a song, a slide show, a video, a story, a skit, or a trick to capture interest. Juggle apples and oranges to show how your company must juggle its priorities in order to maintain a healthy operation. Toss a ball to a participant and have that person ask a question or make a statement regarding the objective for the meeting. Once done, that participant throws the ball to someone else to add another thought. Bring in an umbrella or a children's plastic wading pool to illustrate umbrella operations or pooling together. Dress up as Ben Franklin to make a point about diplomacy and invention in a global market. Read a children's story to illustrate a quality. Use your imagination to capture the participants' imaginations.

Use props, music, a song, a slide show, a video, a story, a skit, or a trick to capture interest.

◆ Use a forced analogy to stimulate creative thinking. "How is our service or product like an animal, a snack, an automobile, or a candle?"

◆ Add the number of years of working experience each participant has and announce the total. Add their ages minus the number of participants to find the total number of years of communication experience. Build confidence that with the sum of their experience, participants will successfully face the main issue presented in the meeting.

7

75

◆ Post butcher paper along one wall of the room. Invite each participant to draw or write one thing that contributes to the total vision of the group. This creative brainstorming technique gets people and ideas moving.

◆ Ask each participant to select a numbered playing card from a basket. The person must contribute during the meeting at least the number of times shown on the card.

◆ Make a promise at the beginning of the meeting to end on time.

◆ Record each current problem, concern, or conflict on a separate sheet of paper. Wad each into a ball or make each into a paper airplane. Sail one at a time to a participant. Team up participants to list possible resolutions, and later report them to the entire group.

◆ Refer to the last meeting's conclusion, either its decisions or its closing exercise. Tie in the opening for this meeting with the end of the last one.

Use the following lists of tips to make unusual introductions of leaders and participants, and to give clear, concise instructions. Both techniques will grab your audience's attention.

Making Introductions

If you're introducing a superior or a speaker, you'll want to ensure the audience's attention and appreciation during the presentation. This is a matter of professional courtesy. Besides, if someone else is doing the presenting, you get to relax, and that deserves proper acknowledgment!

All of these ideas are effective openers. Remember that the opener is actually the first transition in your meeting, the one between the outer world of daily activity and the inner world of the meeting. Some of these ideas may also be effective transitions between activities and agenda items during the meeting. They encourage and maintain enthusiasm.

Tips for Making Introductions

◆ Take a sip of water and then pause before introducing yourself or others. Lubricate your throat and collect your thoughts.

◆ Make an important introduction approximately five minutes into the opening. Set the context for your participants by identifying reasons and ways to remember this person. People remember a name better after they have information and a face to associate the name with.

◆ Provide participants with written biographies of main presenters. Photographs posted on a bulletin board are also helpful.

Provide participants with written biographies of main presenters.

◆ List significant life experiences of a guest speaker on a transparency, and project it during the introduction. Include information your guest supplies, such as ancestral background, unusual noncareer jobs, family members' occupations or interests, hobbies, and personal successes. For example, introduce a speaker as "a member of a family who owns a crafts business, one of nine children who has one child, a former clam digger, an expert sandwich chef, a frustrated volleyball enthusiast, a Cherokee-Ukrainian-American, and a student of tightrope walking."

◆ Give participants three minutes to discover something unusual about a partner or something good that happened to them that week. Use the information to introduce each other to the group.

◆ Ask each participant to sign in on a transparency projected on the wall. Each then states an expectation for the meeting. Once the names are recorded, the group could analyze the handwriting!

7

◆ If you have a large, diverse group, ask people to stand or to raise hands in response to interesting questions, such as "How many of you have attended a meeting already today?" or "How many of you were born in this state?" or "How many of you remember when this company was first established?" Make sequential statements, such as "Stand if you have worked here for at least two years. Remain standing if you've been here for five years . . . for 10 years . . ." Those who feel protective of their privacy may, of course, silently refrain from participating.

Tips for Giving Instructions

Much time is wasted in meetings due to inadequate instructions. Frustration mounts when people don't know what to do or how to do it. People will judge your entire preparation on how you give directions. Build their confidence in you and save time by stating clear, concise instructions the first time.

Ask participants to do only three or fewer tasks in sequence.

◆ Ask participants to do only three or fewer tasks in sequence. People get more confused as you add tasks because they begin thinking about or doing the first while you're describing the last. Keep instructions simple for best results, or be prepared to explain them again!

◆ Give both spoken and written instructions for clarity and reference.

◆ Tie in the instructions to the rationale or the desired results. Show how what you're asking the participants to do will impact the objective of the meeting.

◆ Ask for questions and be ready to clarify any directions you've given.

You will begin at the scheduled time, but experienced leaders caution you to begin with an item or activity of interest, yet one that is not the most essential. This accommodates late arrivals, while acknowledging those participants who have arrived on time. It also acts as a warm-up for the real task ahead. Usually, the most effective sequence of elements is opener first, then introductions and instructions last. Creating movement and excitement during the opening moments will ensure a good meeting.

Increasing Your Credibility

Every segment of every chapter you've read in this book so far will enhance your credibility. How believable and trustworthy you are depends on your audience's perception of your confidence, commitment, and competence. If your audience members don't perceive these qualities, they will withhold their attention and their commitment. You may be honest, caring, and skilled, but if your audience doesn't think you are, you're sunk! Review the list of ideas on the next page and check any that you intend to use during your next meeting.

> You may be honest, caring, and skilled, but if your audience doesn't think you are, you're sunk!

Ways to Increase Your Credibility

◆ Start meetings on time.

◆ Be well prepared.

◆ Make your answers short and direct.

◆ Use concrete, colorful comparisons.

◆ Use strong action verbs.

◆ Give specific examples.

◆ Define terms, problems, and instructions.

◆ Avoid frequent blinking.

◆ Avoid answering an inappropriate question by directing a question back to the questioner.

◆ Think before you speak.

◆ Keep the discussion in control and focused.

◆ Listen without interrupting, and keep a list of key words each speaker says to keep track of the discussion.

◆ Check interpretations of people's statements for accuracy and clarification.

7

◆ Restate your understanding of a statement, and ask for clarification.

◆ Summarize periodically to highlight significant points.

◆ Identify consequences of each decision.

◆ Facilitate the plan for action.

◆ Establish a clear time limit and end on time.

◆ Acknowledge the value or truth of comments even if you do not agree with them.

◆ Ask the quiet participant for a comment or an opinion.

◆ Make direct eye contact with those who are speaking.

Break eye contact and redirect the discussion if someone is dominating the talk.

◆ Break eye contact and redirect the discussion if someone is dominating the talk.

◆ Remain calm, even if someone is hostile toward you.

◆ Ask someone who is dominating the discussion by repeating a point over and over to record a statement for the minutes or write it on a flip chart. That way, everyone is sure it is physically recorded and mentally noted.

◆ Ask the group to verify information.

◆ Use people's names when you address them.

◆ Defuse any verbal attacks on or toward any participant.

◆ Tell the truth without exaggeration, sarcasm, ridicule, or excuse.

◆ Walk among the participants rather than hide behind a lectern or a table.

◆ Check your facial and body expressions to make sure they're consistent with your words.

- Avoid upward inflections that make your statements sound like questions.

- Check your tone, pitch, and volume.

- Avoid disclaimers, such as "I may be wrong," and tags, such as ". . . don't you?"

- Use multisensory language and activities.

- Take ownership for your mistakes.

- End on time.

Your meeting is now under way, and you are delivering the content. You're conducting an effective, efficient meeting. Your participants are attentive and enthusiastic. And you are competent and confident!

You have now finished the most demanding phase of planning and conducting a meeting. The communication skills you used while speaking and listening to your team kept you focused on both the meeting objective and the process.

Documenting the Meeting

After going to all of this trouble, it would be a shame to neglect a record of your successful meeting! Some meetings need more documentation than others, yet you'll want all of them recorded in some way. Your records prove that you've earned your paycheck by accomplishing your meeting objectives. Your records also show what decisions have been made by whom, as well as what actions have been taken. These records may be used as legal documents, so they must be accurate.

7

Five Ways to Record Meetings

◆ Notes ranging from an annotated agenda to traditional minutes written by an observer, such as a group secretary.

◆ Annotated visuals, such as transparencies and flip charts, which are created during the meeting by the leader or other group representative.

◆ Audiotape.

◆ Videotape.

◆ Transcription of every word said during the meeting.

The method of documentation you select will depend on your resources and needs. Usually, notes written by an individual who represents the group are sufficient. The amount of detail in the notes will vary depending on how detail-oriented the note taker is. If the meeting is short and simple, a few notes under each agenda item will work. If the meeting is more complicated, additional notes identifying decision makers and topics of discussion become more necessary. Agenda items, decisions, and actions provide the outline of the record.

The method of documentation you select will depend on your resources and needs.

Taking notes is easily affordable and doable. Paper, pen, patience, a quick ear, and a speedy hand are the only tools! If you plan to enter the notes into a computer after the meeting is over, consider having a computer in the meeting room where the notes can be entered on the spot.

In many cases, you will be responsible for recording the meeting yourself. Ask for help in taking notes during discussions so that you can pace the meeting and participate as much as possible. Remember that you are also responsible for directing the content and the group dynamics. If the meeting is small and short, you can probably manage to record decisions and actions on your own agenda. Jot down key words to remind you later about important information to record.

When you get back to your office and the computer, add your notes to your list of agenda questions. If you included an action plan format at the bottom of your agenda, that information is now a summary of the follow-up you'll need to do. An example of a format for actions and decisions is a fill-in statement such as this:

"Who_____does what_____by when_____"
       (name)   (action)   (date)

During the meeting, fill in the blanks with the dated plan and the names of those who agreed to complete them.

The LAW Method

Now, we're ready for the meeting to start—on time, of course! The note taker will find this job easier to manage by using the LAW method:

♦ *Listen* first.

♦ *Ask* questions to get the needed answers recorded accurately.

♦ *Write* fast.

Knowing what to write before dividing concentration between note taking and listening will improve accuracy. An audio recording of the meeting can be replayed for crucial wording in decisions.

Even after the meeting ends, several tasks remain. Type the minutes using agenda items as headings, and send them to members for their review before the next meeting. Only then is the meeting really over!

> Knowing what to write before dividing concentration between note taking and listening will improve accuracy.

7

Chapter *Eight*

Finishing the Meeting

Chapter Objectives

▶ Master eight techniques for closing a meeting.

▶ Network after the meeting.

Once you've delivered the content, the hard part is over. What remains are the closing, follow-through, follow-up, and beginning of the next meeting. If you made a presentation during the meeting, you acted out a scene in the play. After reaching the climax of the content, you're back to the job of director. This chapter will show you how to complete one meeting and begin preparing for the next one.

You'll want participants to leave the meeting with a positive sense of accomplishment and a renewed sense of commitment.

Are you beginning to suspect that planning and conducting meetings are never-ending? Good business practices never end, and neither do business meetings. However, you've made great strides toward the most productive meeting ever held by making it this far into the book! Your determination and dedication will drive you toward success!

You'll want participants to leave the meeting with a positive sense of accomplishment and a renewed sense of commitment. For that to happen, the closing exercise must enlighten, entertain, or both. Several ideas follow.

Closing a Meeting

Finding closure allows your team a few minutes to assess the meeting objective one more time. Equally as important is acting as a community one more time. The rapport that develops after working together in this meeting will carry over until the next meeting.

◆ Summarize or ask someone else to summarize the main points and decisions of the meeting.

◆ Distribute a brief values survey, and promise to have the composite ready for the next meeting. Use the HIDDEN Agenda, for instance. Write the key words on a flip chart and ask each participant to rank the six items, high to low, on a 3"-by-5" index card. Collect the cards in a tray beside the exit. Tally the rankings and list them on the chart for the next meeting. Use the results as a greeting or an opener.

◆ Conduct a round-robin activity in which each participant is asked to respond to the team gives everyone the center stage for at least one moment before adjournment. Here are a few ways to stimulate a round robin.

Ask each member to say what she or he learned.

■ "I learned that this group thinks like a team!"
"I learned a new way to approach the accounting department."
"I learned that working together is more fun and more productive."

Invite each participant to give a personal affirmation.

■ "I am capable."
"I will complete all five miles of the Corporate Challenge Run!"

Invite each to give an appreciation for a team member.

■ "I appreciate Jack for asking me about my opinion today."
"I appreciate Kay for pushing us to think of fresh options."

> **Finding closure allows your team a few minutes to assess the meeting objective one more time.**

8

◆ End with a brief evaluation, such as "What was the most helpful part of this meeting?" Ask each member to write a short answer on a sticky note or an index card to leave on or by the door on the way out.

◆ End with a laugh.

◆ Ask for a stand-up evaluation of the meeting: stand up to show a high level of effectiveness, remain seated for average, and kneel for low level. The symbolism will probably get some laughs as everyone rises to exit!

◆ Ask everyone to stand, stretch for six seconds, and clap four times. Then bow and say, "Thank you for that standing ovation!"

◆ Stop the timer or alarm. If you set the clock at the beginning of the meeting, it will either interrupt you at midsentence or your audience will be counting down the final 10 seconds!

After the Meeting

While your impressions are still fresh, jot down observations to improve or include for the next meeting.

Network with individuals after the meeting. Use this valuable time to learn about others' lives, careers, skills, awards, and preferences. These insights will prove helpful as you plan other meetings. Thank support personnel for their help in planning the meeting, and presenters for their efforts in conducting the meeting. Thank yourself for a job well done by treating yourself to a token reward.

Within an hour after the meeting ends, while your impressions are still fresh, jot down observations to improve or include for the next meeting. Keep a log that includes your thoughts and feelings about your meetings: settings, participants, comments, and any other information of interest. Record names of resource people, sketches of seating arrangements, and training strategies that worked or didn't work, promises you or others made, descriptions of openers and closings, action plans with time frames, and names of participants who voiced concerns you want to hear more about. Use your log to guide you in following through on commitments you've made to individuals or groups. This log will help you and the recorder fill in gaps in the minutes, improve communication with team members between meetings, and remind you how much better your meetings are getting each time. The log will also demonstrate your determination and dedication during your next performance review! You can show that you are both people-oriented and results-oriented as you give a progress report on your meetings from one year to the next.

Within a day's time, begin a tentative agenda for a follow-up meeting. List old business and new business before you forget or get sidetracked. Write thank-you notes to key contributors and helpful members. Begin periodic check-in calls to those members who are working on the action plan or on any other decisions made during the meeting, and to those members who missed the meeting. Ask for feedback from friends who attended the meeting. Evaluate the group's performance, your performance, other leaders' performances, and the overall production of the meeting. Set personal goals to achieve during the next meeting cycle.

Sometimes it's impossible to know where one meeting ends and the next begins. Tying up all of the loose ends of this meeting will help you determine if there is enough need to plan a follow-up meeting soon. A good meeting leader stays in contact with team members to maintain communication so that future meetings run smoothly. See how you're doing in this phase of your meeting planning.

> **Evaluate the group's performance, your performance, other leaders' performances, and the overall production of the meeting.**

8

Completion Checklist

Meeting Date: _____ **Meeting Objective:** _____

Task   **Completed/Not Necessary**

                                                           (X)   (N/A)

Selected a closing   _____

Networked   _____

Thanked the support staff   _____

Thanked the contributors   _____

Returned property   _____

Rewarded myself   _____

Wrote in my journal   _____

Started the next agenda   _____

Distributed the minutes or summary memo   _____

Made check-in calls to absentees   _____

Made check-in calls to those involved in the
  action plan   _____

Asked for feedback   _____

Evaluated   _____

Set personal goals   _____